P9-DDW-899

EXPLORING SCIENCE

E R O S I O N

HOW LAND FORMS, HOW IT CHANGES

BY DARLENE R. STILLE

Content Adviser: Jim Walker, Professor of Geology and
Environmental Geosciences, Northern Illinois University

Science Adviser: Terrence E. Young Jr., M.Ed., M.L.S.,
Jefferson Parish (Louisiana) Public School System

Reading Adviser: Susan Kesselring, M.A., Literacy Educator,
Rosemount-Apple Valley-Eagan (Minnesota) School District

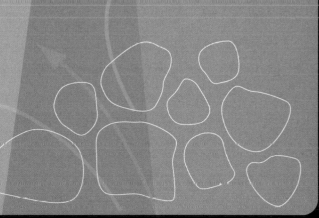

 Compass Point Books • Minneapolis, Minnesota

Compass Point Books • 151 Good Counsel Drive • P.O. Box 669 • Mankato, MN 56002-0669

 This book was manufactured with paper containing at least 10 percent post-consumer waste.

Photographs ©: Tom Bean/Corbis, cover; F. Suchel/Peter Arnold, Inc., 4; Digital Vision, 5, 30; Weatherstock/Peter Arnold, Inc., 6; Charlotte Thege/Peter Arnold, Inc., 8; NASA/GRIN, 9; Richard Hamilton Smith, 11; Tom Murphy/Peter Arnold, Inc., 12; Sharon Gerig/Tom Stack & Associates, 13; Jim Wark/Peter Arnold, Inc., 15, 38; Photodisc, 16–17, 41; John Kieffer/Peter Arnold, Inc., 18; USDA Natural Resources Conservation Service, 19; Lynn Betts, USDA Natural Resources Conservation Service, 20; David L. Brown/Tom Stack & Associates, 21; Robert Galbraith/Peter Arnold, Inc., 23; Norbert Wu/Peter Arnold, Inc., 25; Frans Lemmens/Peter Arnold, Inc., 26; Franklin D. Roosevelt Library, 27; Vincent Dedet/Peter Arnold, Inc., 29; Jorgen Schytte/Peter Arnold, Inc., 31; Freelance Consulting Services Pty Ltd/Corbis, 32; Michael Sewell/Peter Arnold, Inc., 33; Clyde H. Smith/Peter Arnold, Inc., 36; Jeff Greenberg/Unicorn Stock Photos, 39; Mark Edwards/Peter Arnold, Inc., 42; Alex S. MacLean/Peter Arnold, Inc., 43; Luiz C. Marigo/Peter Arnold, Inc., 44; James P. Rowan, 46.

Art Director: Keith Griffin
Managing Editor: Catherine Neitge
Editor: Nadia Higgins
Photo Researcher: Marcie C. Spence
Designer/Page production: The Design Lab
Lead Designer: Jaime Martens
Illustrator: Farhana Hossain
Educational Consultant: Diane Smolinski

Library of Congress Cataloging-in-Publication Data
Stille, Darlene R.
  Erosion : how land forms, how it changes / by Darlene R. Stille.
    p. cm. — (Exploring science)
  Includes bibliographical references and index.
  ISBN 978-0-7565-0854-8 (hardcover)
  ISBN 978-0-7565-1100-5 (paperback)
  1. Erosion—Juvenile literature. I. Title. II. Series.
  QE571.S78 2004
  551.3'02—dc22   2004023077

Visit Compass Point Books on the Internet at www.compasspointbooks.com or e-mail your request to custserv@compasspointbooks.com

About the Author

Darlene R. Stille is a science writer and author of more than 70 books for young people. When she was in high school, she fell in love with science. While attending the University of Illinois, she discovered that she also loved writing. She was fortunate enough to find a career as an editor and writer that allowed her to combine both of her interests. Darlene Stille now lives and writes in Michigan.

TABLE OF CONTENTS ⊕

CHAPTER ONE

The Power of Erosion

THE MAJESTIC PEAK of a snow-covered mountain slowly disappears. A tiny crack in a flat plain grows deeper and wider until it becomes a mighty gorge. A river carves a deep canyon into layers of colorful rock.

Erosion is constantly changing, creating, and erasing features on Earth's surface. Through the power of wind, water, and huge rivers of ice known as glaciers, erosion paints beautiful landscapes.

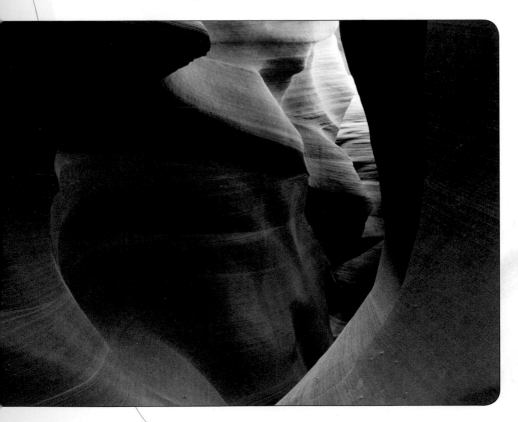

Erosion carved this slot canyon out of colorful sandstone.

Sometimes the process of erosion is incredibly slow, taking hundreds of thousands—even millions—of years. Slow change to a hillside can come from the drip and splash of rainwater. Just as sandpaper scrapes away wood, wind can slowly scrape the rocks off a mountain. Millions of tons of rock and gravel can be picked up and moved piece by piece by the icy underside of a glacier.

Ruth Glacier, Alaska, is a slow-moving river of ice.

Sometimes the changes are sudden. The blasting winds and raging seas of a hurricane rip sand from a beach, and the beach suddenly disappears. With a great roar, the soil on the side of a hill soaked by flooding rains can tear away and crash to a valley below.

Erosion also helps give us soil, which forms from weathered rocks. Erosion moves soil from one place to another. Wind

During a hurricane, fierce winds drive ocean water onto the shore. This rapid rise in sea level, or storm surge, is one of the most destructive aspects of a hurricane.

erosion, for example, deposited fine silt (mineral particles in soil) on the area that became the Great Plains of the Midwestern United States. The silt helped make excellent soil for planting crops. Water erosion by the Mississippi River carried sediments southward to the mouth of the river, creating rich farmland in the Mississippi Delta.

But erosion is not without its problems. People have speeded up erosion in certain places and turned this natural process into a problem. Farming can be a major cause of soil erosion. Each year, the planet loses billions of acres of rich topsoil because of poor farming methods all over the world.

Cutting down trees also causes erosion. The roots of trees hold soil in place. If all the trees on a mountain or hillside are cut down, rainwater running downhill can wash the soil away.

FAST FACT: Worms, insects, snakes, and small mammals dig up and crawl around in the top layers of soil. They are a major cause of erosion because they loosen the soil, which allows it to be carried away by blowing wind and rainwater. Even so, one rainstorm falling on a freshly plowed farm field causes more erosion than all the animals living there could cause in more than 100 years.

Overgrazing of land by cattle causes erosion. Too many cattle, and also cattle left on rangeland too long, will eat almost all the plants, exposing the soil. When the soil dries out, the wind picks it up and carries it away.

We have long heard about the dangers of air pollution and seen the effects of smog floating above a city. We are aware of water pollution and how important it is to keep our lakes and rivers clean. Soil erosion, however, is a silent problem. It is not easy to see soil slipping away from fields.

It may be hard to understand the dangers of losing soil every year. However, it takes thousands of years for rich topsoil to form, and this vital resource is being lost faster than nature can replace it. Without soil, there can be no food. To stop soil erosion, everyone must be aware of this danger. Aware citizens can help scientists and government officials come up with plans to save the soil.

The soil has eroded around this tree in Kenya, leaving its roots exposed.

Erosion on Mars

Erosion can change how an entire planet looks. Erosion by wind, water, and glaciers has changed the surface of Earth many times. Could erosion also have changed the surface of Mars?

Ever since astronomers first looked at Mars through telescopes in the 1700s, they have wondered whether there was water on the Red Planet. After the Space Age began in the mid-1900s, astronomers sent unmanned spacecraft to take close-up pictures of the planet's surface. They found that Mars has channels, gullies, and canyons even deeper than the Grand Canyon. They also saw evidence that sediments had built up in the canyons, channels, and gullies.

text continued on page 10

On September 3, 1976, the unmanned spacecraft *Viking 2* landed on Mars' Utopian Plain.

9

continued from page 9

It looked like sudden floods had eroded these features. And there was something else: Scientists saw evidence of sediments deposited on low, flat plains. Geologists knew that on Earth, erosion by water causes these kinds of features.

However, none of the spacecraft found any evidence of water on Mars. The planet looked bone dry. Mars today is so cold that water would turn to ice. The air, or atmosphere, of Mars is so thin that liquid water would immediately evaporate. The mystery deepened.

However, scientists were convinced that water had to have caused the erosion on Mars. They kept looking for evidence until they found it in 2002. They discovered huge amounts of ice locked up below the surface of Mars. Since then, spacecraft have been finding more and more evidence that there was—and may still be—water on Mars.

The finding raises many more questions. Was Mars once warmer than it is now? If so, could there have been life on Mars? Where is the liquid water now? Is it locked up by the ice under the surface of Mars? Could "ice dams" be holding it back? If so, and an ice dam breaks, liquid water could surge out over the Martian surface, carving channels and gullies just as it does on Earth. Then, because of the cold temperatures and thin atmosphere, the liquid water might disappear as suddenly as it came, leaving nothing but the footprint of its erosion.

CHAPTER TWO

The Erosion Process

EROSION BREAKS UP rocks and soil and moves the pieces to another place. The first step in the process of natural erosion begins with the weathering of rocks. Blowing wind can wear down rocks. Water can dissolve minerals in rocks, and plant roots can break rocks apart.

One of the main causes of weathering is freezing and thawing. Rainwater seeps into cracks in a block of solid rock. The water freezes into ice. When water turns to ice, it expands. The ice in the crack pushes hard enough against the surrounding rock to split the rock apart. Further weathering breaks the rock into smaller and smaller pieces.

The pieces eventually become small enough to be moved by water, wind, or glacial ice. The pieces of eroded rock set off on a long, downhill journey. They are pulled along by the force of gravity.

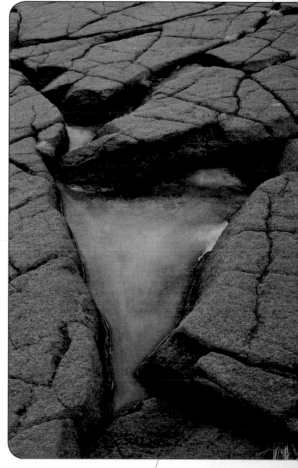

Ice breaks apart thick slabs of rock.

ONE EROSION STORY

On a high mountaintop, wind and water break up pieces of solid rock. The pieces of rock have nowhere to go but down. They could be carried downhill by rainwater or melted snow, or they could just slide down in an avalanche.

FAST FACT: Rockslides and landslides erode large chunks of land on mountains. This type of erosion is called mass movement.

Huge amounts of snow, ice, soil, and rock barrel down a mountain during an avalanche.

Either way, the pieces of rock land in a stream at the bottom of the mountain. Water in the stream picks up and carries the smallest pieces and rolls the bigger pieces along the streambed to a valley far below.

In the valley, the pieces of rock erode even more until they become tiny particles of sand, silt, or clay. They join with particles from decayed plants or animals to form soil. Plants begin to grow in the soil and send their roots deep down.

Then, there is a season of unusually heavy rainfall. A river flowing through the valley becomes swollen with floodwaters. The waters spill over the riverbanks and flood the valley. The floodwaters carry tons and tons of the soil away.

Floodwaters cause erosion when they pick up soil and carry it away.

The rushing, muddy river water carries the soil particles to a faraway lake, where they sink to the bottom and become part of the sediment. Creatures living in the lake die and get buried in the sediment.

Over millions of years, the sediment turns to rock. During this time, the lake dries up, and the land becomes a desert. Not far away, however, another river forms. At first, it's just a trickle flowing across the desert after the spring rains. The water begins to carve a streambed, and it grows deeper and wider every year, until it becomes a swift-flowing river.

The riverbed deepens into a canyon, exposing layers of sedimentary rock. Once again, the particles from the mountain-top, now part of the sedimentary rock, are exposed to the forces of erosion. Buried among the rocks are fossils of animals and plants that died millions of years ago and settled to the bottom of the ancient lake. The exposed canyon walls erode further over millions of years.

At times, wind blows fiercely through the steep-walled canyon carved by the river. The wind picks up sand particles and blows them against the canyon walls. The blowing wind sandblasts the canyon walls. The wind exposes particles from the ancient mountaintop and carries the particles thousands of miles to another river that flows to the sea. The journey of erosion from a mountaintop to the bottom of the sea is completed.

This, however, is only one way that erosion can occur. There are many other erosion stories caused by water, wind, and glaciers.

Marble Canyon, Arizona, was formed over millions of years by the forces of wind and water.

The Grand Canyon of the Colorado River

The riders in the rubber raft can hear the roar of the approaching white-water rapids. They hang on tightly to safety ropes as their craft sweeps through the water, rushing over boulders and rocks on the bed of the Colorado River. What a thrill to feel the power of this mighty river!

The Colorado begins in the Rocky Mountains of Colorado and flows 1,450 miles (2,334 kilometers) down into Mexico. Along the way, it passes through the Grand Canyon in northern Arizona, a canyon that the river carved out over millions of years.

By studying layers of rocks in the canyon, geologists have determined that the river began to erode the walls about 6 million years ago. Slowly, the flowing water cut through layer after layer of rock—layers of limestone, sandstone, and shale.

Eventually, the river eroded a canyon that is 277 miles (446 km) long, about 1 mile (1.6 km) deep, and in one place 18 miles (29 km) wide. The same river that is so much fun to raft on is still cutting through rock, still eroding this great canyon.

White-water rafters rush along the Colorado River, past the walls of the Grand Canyon.

How Does Water Cause Erosion?

EROSION BY WATER can affect many landscapes. In addition to carving riverbeds and canyons, water washes the upper layers of soil off of farm fields and causes beach erosion.

There are patterns to the ways in which water can erode farmland. Among the main soil erosion patterns are sheet erosion and rill erosion.

Water flowing downhill erodes a rocky hillside.

SHEET EROSION

Sheet erosion is caused by raindrops loosening and stripping the rich top layer of soil off of a field. This form of erosion is the most difficult type to see.

In sheet erosion, raindrops act like tiny bombs landing on the soil. These raindrops blast out silt and clay, the lighter soil particles, near the surface. On even a slight slope, the rainwater that the soil cannot absorb runs off the surface and carries with it the soil particles that have been knocked out of place. The slope of the land determines how much runoff from sheet erosion will occur. The steeper and longer the slope, the more soil will be carried away.

Plants growing in the soil provide shelter from the raindrops. In early spring, however, the soil has been just recently tilled and planted. The young plants are not big enough to give the soil much protection from heavy spring rains. Therefore, a great deal of sheet erosion occurs at this time.

In sheet erosion, raindrops blast the soil's surface. Because sheet erosion happens gradually, it is often difficult to detect.

RILL EROSION

Sometimes rainwater runoff carves small channels into the soil surface. These channels, called rills, are like miniature streambeds. If the runoff goes on for a long time, the rainwater carves deeper and deeper rills. Long, steep slopes and bare, loose soil also help the process along.

A network of rills spreads out over hilly farmland. Rills usually suggest that the land is also suffering from sheet erosion.

When the rills become deep and wide enough, they are called gullies. During a downpour, a large amount of soil can be eroded because of rills and gullies. Gullies can become so deep and wide that farmers cannot drive their tractors over them.

Plowing a field evens the soil surface, which can temporarily slow rill erosion. However, plowing also loosens the soil, making

Tree branches have been piled into a gully in order to slow further erosion.

it easier for new rills to form in the future. As with sheet erosion, plants can offer protection from rill erosion, but the same problems occur each spring when the plants are young and the field is newly plowed.

POLLUTION FROM RUNOFF

Not only does runoff carry away rich topsoil, it also removes chemical fertilizers and pesticides applied to the soil. The runoff carries these chemicals downhill to pollute streams and rivers. It can also seep into and pollute groundwater.

Water polluted with fertilizers and pesticides must be cleaned before people can drink it, and this process is very expensive. Also, algae grow wildly in lakes polluted with chemical fertilizers. These so-called algal blooms set off a complex chain reaction. The algae block sunlight and use up oxygen. The low oxygen conditions encourage bacteria that produce sulfur and other chemicals, eventually killing the fish and other animals that live there. The rotting animals and algae turn the lake into a foul-smelling mess.

BEACH EROSION

Beach erosion occurs along shorelines of lakes and oceans. This kind of erosion both creates and destroys beaches. Waves, tides, and underwater currents pick up and carry sand from one place

to another. The water can erode sand from one beach, making it smaller, while it deposits sand on another beach, making it bigger. Beach erosion is part of a natural process.

An algal bloom has destroyed wildlife at Lake Champlain in Quebec, Canada.

Fossils and Erosion

We may never have known about dinosaurs if it hadn't been for erosion. The forces of erosion helped preserve dead dinosaurs and other plants and animals as fossils. Then the forces of erosion helped uncover the fossils.

Fossils are the preserved remains of ancient plants and animals or impressions left in stone by the plants and animals after they died. Footprints and other signs of plants and animals are also fossils. Many fossils of dinosaurs and other animals are locked up in sedimentary rock.

The fossil of one such dinosaur formed when the animal died in a place that was soon covered by water. The dinosaur's skin and internal organs decayed. But water brought in sediments that buried the dinosaur's skeleton. Little by little, minerals in water replaced material dissolving out of the bones.

Over millions of years, layer after layer of sediment built up. Pressure from the weight of the upper layers turned the lower layers to rock. The hard, mineral bones of the dead dinosaur remained in the sedimentary rock for millions more years.

The climate where the dinosaur had died underwent several changes. The dinosaur lived and died in a lush tropical forest. Eventually, the forest was buried by water and became the bottom of a sea. Over time, the sea dried up, leaving a dry wasteland.

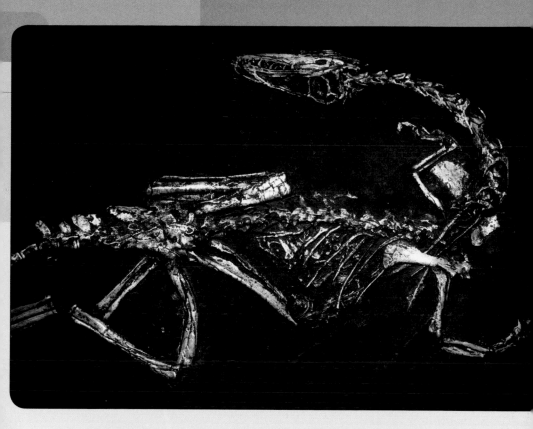

Then one day, erosion went to work again. A stream of water began cutting through the dry land. As it cut deeper, it created a gorge. The walls of the gorge were striped with layer upon layer of sediment, and in that sediment were the teeth and bones of a huge dinosaur that walked on Earth as long as 230 million years ago.

Paleontologists find the oldest fossils in the lowest layers of sedimentary rock. These are the layers of rock that formed first. The top layers of sedimentary rock formed last, so these contain the youngest fossils. Paleontologists trace how plants and animals evolved by comparing the fossils in each layer.

Erosion uncovered the fossilized bones of a dinosaur trapped in sedimentary rock.

How Does Wind Cause Erosion?

W I N D cannot pick up big rocks or boulders and blow them to a new location. Wind works on smaller particles, such as bits of soil and grains of sand. Nevertheless, wind is a powerful force of erosion. It lifts the smallest particles into the air and rolls the larger particles along the ground.

Wind is the main cause of erosion in deserts and dry lands, where water is scarce. Dry soil with few plants to hold it in place can easily be eroded by the wind. In the Sahara desert of northern Africa, fierce winds constantly shift mountains of sand called dunes.

Wind causes shifting sand dunes in the Sahara desert of northern Africa.

WIND EROSION DURING DROUGHTS

Wind erosion can also blow away soil in places that are not usually
dry. During times of drought—when little or no rain falls for a long
period of time—even rich soil can dry out and plants can die.

Farmers who lived in Colorado, Kansas, New Mexico, Okla-
homa, and Texas during the 1930s experienced the devastating
combination of wind erosion and drought. At times, dust clouds
of rich topsoil blown off the land were thick enough to cause
darkness in the middle of the day. This area came to be known
as the Dust Bowl.

A dust storm in Rolla, Kansas, in 1935

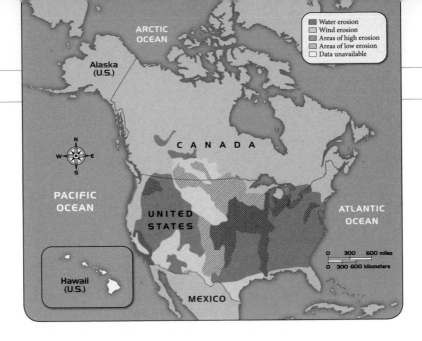

The world was in the grip of a terrible economic depression when the trouble began. The drought parched the soil. The wind blew the dry soil away. The erosion changed the nature of the soil. The wind blew away the lighter particles of silt and organic matter that make the soil fertile. Many families faced poverty as their land was destroyed and they could no longer grow crops.

The drought lasted seven years. In 1934 alone, strong winds blowing from the west picked up about 350 million tons (318

FAST FACT: Erosion by wind is responsible for about 40 percent of the 171.8 million acres (70 million hectares) of soil lost to erosion in the United States each year, according to the U.S. Department of Agriculture.

This map shows areas of the United States and Canada that are most affected either by wind erosion or water erosion.

million metric tons) of soil and swept it through the air all the way to the Atlantic coast. The entire eastern half of the United States was blanketed with a massive dust cloud.

In response to the disaster, the federal government set up the Soil Conservation Service. The service taught farmers ways to protect the soil, including planting more than 18,500 miles (29,800 km) of trees as windbreaks.

It was too late, however, for thousands of farm families, whose land and livelihoods had been destroyed. Many of them packed their remaining belongings and moved west to California.

WIND EROSION ON RANGELAND

Cattle can also contribute to wind erosion. Cattle, sheep, and goats graze on rangeland plants. The animals, especially sheep, can chew and rip up the plants from a large area of land, leaving the soil without protection. When a strong wind comes along, it picks up the dry soil and carries it far away.

A herd of goats has overgrazed a pasture in Chad, Africa, leaving the land exposed to the forces of erosion.

WIND, THE SCULPTOR

Wind can do more than just move sand and soil. It can use those particles blowing in the air to carve up rock. Wind erosion, working with water erosion caused by flash floods, was responsible for the starkly beautiful landforms of the badlands in North Dakota and South Dakota.

The Badlands National Park in South Dakota is known for its thousands of beautiful and interesting landforms.

POLLUTION AND OTHER PROBLEMS
FROM WIND EROSION

Dust particles carried by wind sometimes rise up in the atmosphere. Dust in the air is a form of pollution that can cause eye irritation and breathing problems. It can reduce visibility for pilots and drivers.

Wind causes damaging sandstorms on deserts. The blowing sand can blast the paint off of houses and automobiles. Blowing sand and soil can pile up along fences and cover highways. Sand and soil eroded by the wind can clog up drainage ditches meant to control the flow of rainwater after a storm.

A man covers his face with a scarf during a sandstorm in Niger, Africa.

CHAPTER FIVE

How Do Glaciers Cause Erosion?

TODAY, GLACIERS cover about 10 percent of Earth's surface. During the Ice Age, which ended about 11,500 years ago, glaciers covered far more of Earth's area, covering all of what is now Canada and northern parts of the United States.

Glaciers have caused some of the most extensive erosion on the planet. Though rivers can cut deep canyons into the land, glaciers  can change the landforms of an entire continent. Erosion caused by Ice Age glaciers created some of Earth's most spectacular features, including the U-shaped fjords in Scandinavia and the Great Lakes in North America.

HOW DOES A GLACIER FORM?

A glacier is a vast amount of ice that forms because of snowfall year after year. In order for a glacier to form, more snow must fall in the colder months than melts in the warmer months.

Thousands of years ago, glaciers carved out fjords, such as this one in Norway.

Every year a new layer of snow builds up. The heavy snow layers press down on the layers below. The pressure compacts the snow and turns it into ice, somewhat like when you pack soft snow with your hands and it turns into an icy snowball. When the ice becomes thick enough, the glacier begins to move.

FAST FACT: According to the U.S. National Snow and Ice Data Center, the Kutiah Glacier in Pakistan holds the record for the fastest glacier ever. In 1953, it moved 7.44 miles (12 km) in three months.

Tourists in kayaks take in a spectacular side view of South Sawyer Glacier, Alaska. Large glaciers, such as this one, can be hundreds of feet thick.

WHY DOES A GLACIER MOVE?

The force of gravity pulls a glacier down a slope, just as gravity pulls rocks, soil, and water downhill. Complex things go on inside a glacier to help it move. Ice crystals change their shape. Pressure and friction at the bottom of the glacier causes heat, which makes ice at the bottom of the glacier melt. This meltwater helps the glacier glide along.

When a glacier moves forward, or downhill, geologists say it advances. When a glacier melts and moves backward,

This map shows areas in the Northern Hemishpere that were covered by glaciers during the Ice Age.

geologists say it retreats. It is the movement of glaciers that causes erosion.

HOW CAN A GLACIER'S MOVEMENT
CAUSE EROSION?

First, advancing glaciers can break up rock. Melted water under the glacier seeps down into cracks in the hard rock. The water freezes, the ice expands, and the pressure breaks the rock into smaller pieces.

This map shows areas in the Northern Hemisphere covered by glaciers today.

The pieces of rock become mixed into the ice at the bottom, or base, of the glacier. The base of the glacier is now like a gigantic sanding machine. As the glacier advances, the rocks in the base grind away at the bedrock below. More rocks break off and become mixed into the ice. The glacier causes massive erosion by grinding away more and more rock as it moves.

A glacier can get stuck to bedrock when a lot of ice under the base melts and then refreezes. Gravity keeps tugging on the glacier, however, trying to pull it forward. Eventually, gravity wins, and the glacier moves. Generally, a glacier can move anywhere from about 1 foot (30 centimeters) a year to 1 foot a day. As it moves, it can rip out huge chunks of the bedrock it is stuck to.

Heaps of rocks have been deposited by a glacier.

CHAPTER SIX

Controlling Erosion

THERE ARE TWO SIDES to the erosion story: natural erosion and speeded-up erosion caused by human activities. The answers to questions about controlling erosion depend on which type of erosion is involved.

WHEN SHOULD WE LEAVE EROSION ALONE?

Natural erosion is a process of nature, and there are times when environmental scientists think we can do more harm than good by trying to control it. Beach erosion is one example. Waves and tides in oceans and lakes are constantly moving sand. This process takes sand from one place and deposits it at another, so the movement of water is making new beaches while it erodes others away.

The problem, say environmental scientists, is that people want to build homes near the shore. When lake water levels rise or there are ocean storms with unusually high waves, these homes can be damaged or destroyed. Newspapers carry pictures of beach houses hanging off cliffs or partially underwater.

So homeowners pressure their local governments to do something about the beach erosion problem. Engineers may come in and build seawalls between the homes and the water. They may build break-waters or break walls in the water to ease the

force of waves hitting the shore. They may try to rebuild the beach by bringing in sand.

Scientists say that dumping sand on an eroded beach is probably a waste of effort. The water will simply erode the sand

A house has been propped up on stilts in an attempt to save it from beach erosion.

over and over again. They argue that building seawalls and other structures can actually cause more beach loss than it prevents. By disturbing the natural patterns of waves and currents, the structures keep lake or ocean waters from depositing sand on other beach areas. Instead of forming beaches, the sand might pile up behind piers or be carried out to sea. And so overall more, rather than fewer, beach areas are lost.

Officials attempt to control erosion on a beach in Cape Cod, Massachusetts.

Global Warming and Beach Erosion

Oceanographers (scientists who study the sea) have found a disturbing trend. Sea levels are slowly rising in many parts of the world, which is leading to increased beach erosion. From California to Massachusetts to cliffs along the English coast, scientists have discovered that beach erosion is a growing problem.

Why is the sea level rising? In the opinion of most scientists, the polar ice caps are melting due to global warming.

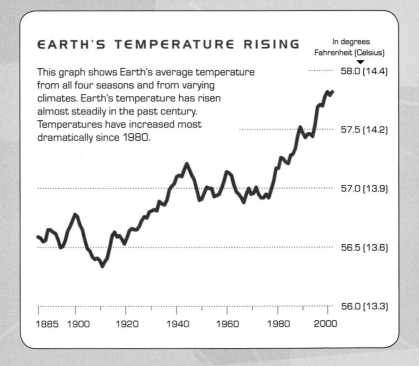

EARTH'S TEMPERATURE RISING

In degrees Fahrenheit (Celsius)

This graph shows Earth's average temperature from all four seasons and from varying climates. Earth's temperature has risen almost steadily in the past century. Temperatures have increased most dramatically since 1980.

58.0 (14.4)

57.5 (14.2)

57.0 (13.9)

56.5 (13.6)

56.0 (13.3)

1885 1900 1920 1940 1960 1980 2000

Global warming is a rise in the average yearly temperature of Earth.

The average temperature of Earth has been rising since the early 1900s. Most scientists believe the rise is due to an increase in the greenhouse effect. Certain so-called greenhouse gases in Earth's atmosphere help keep our planet warm enough to support life. Carbon dioxide and other gases act like the glass in a greenhouse. They keep the sun's heat from escaping into space.

Many scientists believe that human activities are putting too much carbon dioxide into the atmosphere. The carbon dioxide comes mainly from car exhaust fumes and from factories and power plants that burn coal and oil. This excess carbon dioxide is causing an increased greenhouse effect and changing the global climate.

Car exhaust is one of the leading causes of air pollution. It sends carbon dioxide into the atmosphere, increasing the greenhouse effect.

WHEN SHOULD WE CONTROL EROSION?

Erosion caused by farming and other industries is a different matter. Every year, the planet loses million of acres of topsoil. Every year, the population of the world grows by millions of people. According to the Food and Agricultural Organization of the United Nations, the amount of farmland per person has gone down by about one-third since 1951. Imagine what might happen

A dust storm blows topsoil off the land in Ethiopia, Africa.

if one day there was too little soil and too many people. Farmers could not grow enough food to feed the world.

We cannot stop all human activities that cause soil erosion. Farmers must plow up fields to plant food crops. Ranchers must graze sheep and cattle on rangeland. Foresters must cut down trees to make lumber. However, there are ways to continue farming, ranching, and cutting down trees while conserving the soil.

Soil scientists promote a policy called wise use of soil. Farmers can plant stands of trees and other vegetation along the borders of their fields to break the force of the blowing wind. They can plow their fields in patterns that limit erosion by rainwater runoff.

By plowing across a hill, instead of along the slope, farmers can slow the flow of water downhill. This saves soil loss by water erosion.

Ranchers can move their herds around from one place to another on grazing land. This gives the grasses and other plants a chance to grow back. They can limit the number of livestock on a plot of land. This wise use of rangeland prevents the soil from becoming bare and blowing away.

Foresters can immediately plant new trees to replace those cut down for lumber. They can cut down some trees while leaving others standing so that there are always roots to protect the forest soil. They can leave dead branches in place to provide additional protection for the forest soil.

Erosion is a complex issue. By learning more about it, we understand when and how to prevent erosion and when to let this powerful force of nature do its work alone.

People plant trees in Brazil, a country that has been hit hard by loss of forests.

algae—plantlike organisms that live mostly in water

badlands—areas with many small, steep hills and deep gullies

bedrock—a layer of solid rock beneath the layers of soil and loose gravel broken up by weathering

canyons—deep valleys with steep walls usually formed by a stream or river

economic depression—a time when businesses are failing and an unusual number of people are out of work, such as in the 1930s

fertile—good for growing crops

fertilizers—substances that contain nutrients needed by plants

fjords (pronounced fee-yordz)—long, narrow ocean inlets that are surrounded by cliffs or steep slopes

gorge—a canyon with steep walls that rise straight upward

groundwater—water found in underground chambers; it is tapped for drinking water through wells and springs

organic—produced by animals or plants

pesticides—substances, usually chemical, applied to crops to kill harmful insects and other creatures

sedimentary rock—rock formed by layers of sediment being pressed together over thousands or millions of years

sediments—sand, mud, and other materials carried from one place to another by water, wind, or a glacier

topsoil—the top layer of soil that is best for planting

weathering—the breaking up of rocks and soil, mainly by wind and water

▸ To improve rangeland, people sometimes set fire to parts of it. This practice, called prescribed burning, kills poisonous and other unwanted plants. Like weeding, this leaves more room for useful plants. These plants can then flourish and better protect the land from erosion.

▸ Niagara Falls are two giant waterfalls along the Niagara River in upstate New York and Canada. Observers have noticed that this spectacular natural wonder is moving slightly to the east and south. As the river wears away the rocky walls that form its path, the position of the waterfalls is slowly changing year after year.

▸ A natural arch is a rock that juts out of the earth in the shape of an upside-down U or C. It was formed completely by natural erosion. At Arches National Park in Utah, more than 2,000 sandstone arches can be found, including Landscape Arch, one of the largest natural arches in the world. It measures 306 feet (93.3 meters) from base to base.

▸ Most fossils in sedimentary rock are uncovered by erosion. From time to time, however, a fossil is exposed by building projects and oil-well drilling that dig up the earth.

▸ In the deepest layers of the Grand Canyon, paleontologists find fossils of algae that are about a billion years old.

▸ When glacial ice becomes very dense, it turns blue. White glacial ice is a sign that it is filled with tiny air bubbles.

▸ Glaciers contain 75 percent of the planet's fresh water supply.

▸ Dust devils are swirling winds that pop up on deserts. Picking up dust from the desert floor makes dust devils visible. They look like small tornadoes. Dust devils occur on Mars as well as on Earth.

A dust devil makes a column of swirling sand.

Further Reading

Colson, Mary. *Crumbling Earth*. Chicago: Raintree, 2004.
Kallen, Stuart A. *The Grand Canyon*. San Diego: Kidhaven Press, 2003.
Parks, Peggy J. *Sand Dunes*. San Diego: Kidhaven Press, 2004.
Winner, Cherie. *Erosion*. Minneapolis: Carolrhoda Books, 1999.

On the Web

For more information on this topic, use FactHound.
1. Go to *www.facthound.com*
2. Type in this book ID: **0756508541**
3. Click on the *Fetch It* button.
FactHound will find the best Web sites for you.

On the Road

Forest History Center
2609 County Road
Grand Rapids, MN 55744
218/327-4482
To learn about the changing relationship between people and the land in northern Minnesota

Sleeping Bear Dunes National Lakeshore
9922 Front St.
Empire, MI 49630-0797
231/326-5134
To see some beautiful landforms at this national park along Michigan's eastern coastline

Grand Canyon National Park
P.O. Box 129
Grand Canyon, AZ 86023
928/638-7888
To visit one of the world's most spectacular canyons